I0840464

Manatee Coloring Book

Manatee Coloring Book

I LOVE MANATEES, OK?

Manatee Coloring Book

Manatee Coloring Book

Manatee Coloring Book

DRAW A MANATEE!

Copy the 
Manatee in these
small squares...

one square at a time

...into these
bigger squares!

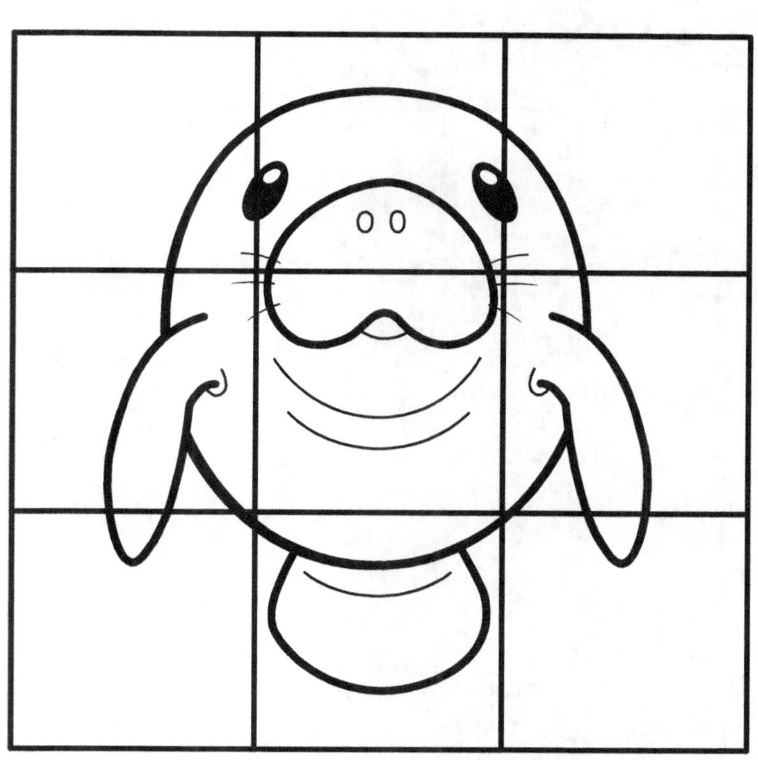

Manatee Coloring Book

Manatee Coloring Book

Manatee Coloring Book

Manatee Coloring Book

FLOATY
POTATO

Manatee Coloring Book

DRAW A MANATEE!

Copy the ➜
Manatee in these
small squares...

one square at a time

...into these ⬇
bigger squares!

Manatee Coloring Book

Manatee Coloring Book

Manatee Coloring Book

Manatee Coloring Book

Manatee Coloring Book

DRAW A TURTLE!

Copy the  →
Turtle in these
small squares...

one square at a time

...into these
bigger squares! ↓

Manatee Coloring Book

Manatee Coloring Book

Manatee Coloring Book

Manatee Coloring Book

MANATEE
HUGS!

Manatee Coloring Book

DRAW A MANTA RAY!

Copy the 
Manta Ray in these
small squares...

one square at a time

...into these
bigger squares!

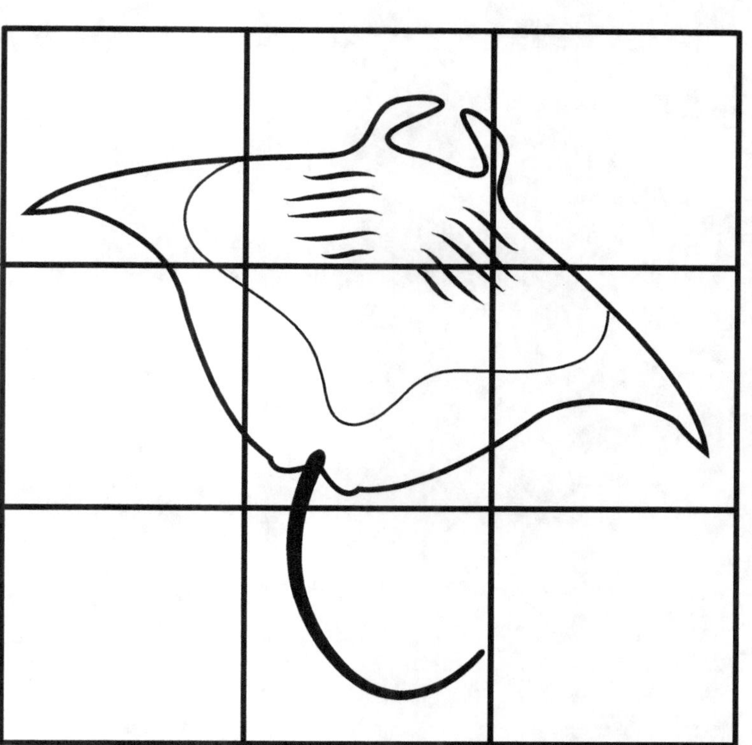

Manatee Coloring Book

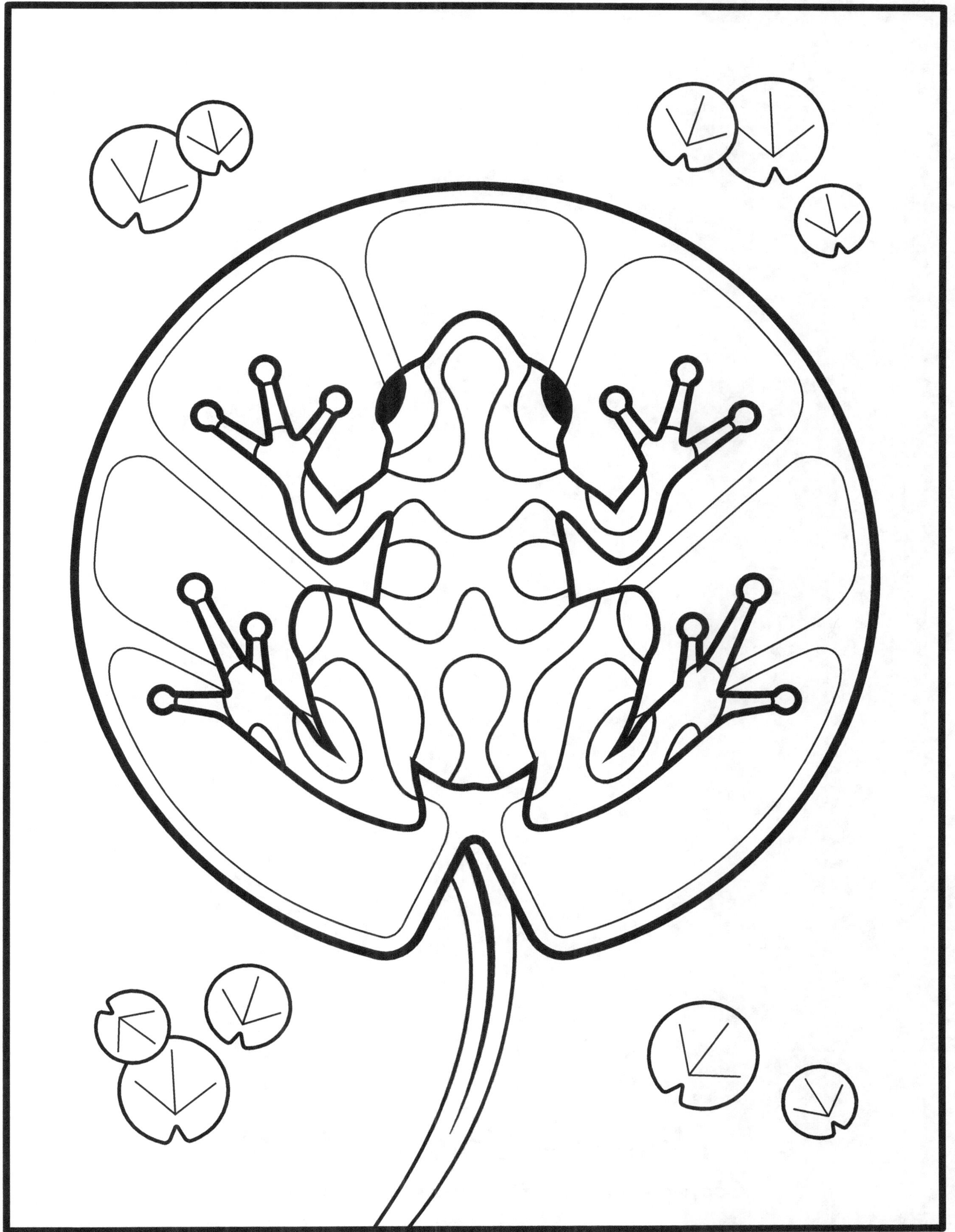

Manatee Coloring Book

Manatee Coloring Book

GOODBYE!

Manatee Coloring Book